Monographic Journals of the Near East *Afroasiatic Linguistics* 7/6 (November 1980)

APHASIC EVIDENCE FOR LEXICAL AND PHONOLOGICAL REPRESENTATIONS

by

Malachi Barkai
English Department
Bar Ilan University
Ramat Gan, Israel

Linguistic phenomena as manifested in the case of a Hebrew-speaking aphasic are discussed in this monograph. The patient's linguistic performance included: (1) writing down forms which deviated from the standard orthography, but which corresponded remarkably well with the types of underlying phonological representation that a linguist might independently propose; (2) verbal behavior which involved the frequently random transfer of verbs from one class to another; (3) restructuring of surface forms to form "novel" roots; (4) errors involving the complex rule of spirantization. Attention is paid to the implications for linguistic research in general, and for Semitic in particular.

TABLE OF CONTENTS

1. INTRODUCTION

Within the last few years, there has been an increasing awareness of the importance of the aphasic paradigm to linguistic research.[1] The study of aphasia can teach us a lot about the nature of normal human speech; it can be an important instrument with which to check the empirical validity of different aspects of linguistic theories (see, for example, Weigl and Bierwisch (1970), Whitaker (1971), Schnitzer (1974)).

This work is concerned with various aspects of linguistic theory, particularly those related to the lexicon, morphology and phonology. After a brief profile of the patient (Section 2), evidence is brought supporting the notion of a morphophonemic level of representation (Sections 3.1 and 3.2). The paper discusses the nature of lexical representations, in the light of both the oral and written errors made by the patient.

The language of the patient is Hebrew. Since this is a Semitic language, there are specific problems relating to the consonantal root. The data show, in a way in which normal performance could not, how the concept of the root was present in the patient's mind.

Furthermore, the patient's correct output of verb-related nouns and nominalized forms is contrasted with his impaired performance in verbs; linguistic and neurological implications are considered (Sections 4 and 7). Mistakes involving obstruent alterations indicate again how an aphasic paradigm may help us resolve purely linguistic hypotheses; in this case, the question of how abstract can phonology be (Section 6). The findings are discussed in the light of other assessments of how aphasic research can support the psychological reality of linguistic hypotheses (Section 7).

Much of this study is an attempt to answer Weigl and Bierwisch's question: "Given the linguistically motivated set of levels for the representation of linguistic structure and the components of grammars, i.e. the semantic, syntactic, morphological and phonological rules, how are these levels of representation and components of grammars motivated from the point of view of their accessibility under pathological conditions?" (1970:2).

2. THE BACKGROUND

The subject is a 33-year-old native speaker of Hebrew, Dudu, who suffered traumatic brain damage in the Arab-Israeli war of October, 1973. Most of the damage, caused by shrapnel, was to the anterior and superior parts of the left parietal lobe; probably the superior part of the frontal lobe, close to the Rolandic fissure, was also affected. His dysgraphia, (see below) suggests that the damage reached the supra-marginal gyrus. He is right-handed and has right hemiplegia.

[1] I wish to take this opportunity to thank the Loewenstein Hospital, Ra'anana for its very kind cooperation and for having permitted me to work with the patient. This work was supported by a grant from the Tel-Aviv University, to which I convey my thanks. I also wish to thank Professors H.A. Whitaker, H. Buckingham, M. Schnitzer, S.A. Schane, R.B. Lees, and C. Parrish for having read an earlier version of the paper and making valuable comments upon it. Any mistakes or oversights, however, are my own.

The brain damage caused a hearing loss, which particularly affected the higher frequencies. There were some syntactic problems but hardly any anomia. Prosodic elements were generally well-preserved.

During the crucial period of his recovery, in particular in January and February, 1974, when most of the errors described here occurred, the patient spoke slowly and clearly enough to enable the researcher to make broad transcriptions of his speech.

Dudu suffered from a mild to moderate form of dysgraphia:

a) he found it difficult to write without having the letters of the alphabet in front of him;
b) he found it difficult to name the letters. Sometimes, he would utter a series of letters to find the one he needed. If, for example, he was seeking the grapheme representing [m], he might begin further back in the Hebrew alphabet, at <k> and continue <l> - <m> ;
c) when writing to dictation, he or the therapist would often have to break up a word into syllables;
d) he often transposed letters, particularly "vav" (representing /u/ or /o/), "jod" (/i/ or /e/)[2] or "reš" (/r/).

On the other hand, he did not often confuse visually similar graphemes. He never inserted unnecessary consonants (this is important for Section 3.2 below).

His dysgraphia can be summed up by saying that, while the process leading to writing a word down was quite laborious, the end product was more often correct than not.

Dudu's treatment of four linguistic phenomena of Hebrew will be described and discussed below. The phenomena are:

a) Metathesis (Section 3.1);
b) Deletion of the initial /h/ of the definite article after certain proclitic prepositions, henceforth referred to as preposition-article-contraction or PAC (Section 3.2);
c) The Semitic root and verb class transfer (Section 5);
d) Spirantization (Section 6).

3. THE LINGUISTIC PHENOMENA OBSERVED

3.1. Metathesis

There is a Hebrew verb prefix of the form /Cit/, which usually denotes reflexivity or mutuality. The initial consonant (C) varies according to tense, person, etc.; we shall use the past tense consonant, /h/. If this morpheme is prefixed to a verb stem (VS) with an initial sibilant, /c, s, š/, there is metathesis between the /t/ of the prefix and the sibilant. Below are a few examples of the Hebrew reflexive verb, with and without metathesis:

[2] Hebrew aphasics often exhibit confusion in their use of these letters. One reason is, no doubt, that the use of "vav" and "yod" as graphemes representing vowels is unusual in an orthography which is basically consonantal. The occasional transposition of these letters must in no way be linked to the systematic and morphophonemically motivated derivation described in Section 3.1.

Initial consonant of VS is not a sibilant:

(1) *hitbager*		'he matured'
(2) *hitmakem*		'he located himself'
(3) *hitlabeš*		'he dressed himself'
(4) *hitnaʾer*		'he shook himself'
etc.		

Initial consonant of VS is a sibilant

(5) *histager*	(*sagar* 'he shut')	'he shut himself in'
(6) *histakem*	(*sikem* 'he added up')	'it totalled'
(7) *hištabeš*	(*šibeš* 'he spoilt')	'it got spoilt'
(8) *hictaʾer*	(*caʾar* 'sorrow')	'he was sorry'
etc.		

There are no exceptions to the metathesis rule, which is productive and restricted morphologically. It is expressed in the spelling system, where the graphemes[3] for /t/ ALWAYS follow the sibilant.

The patient was asked to write down a list of words chosen by the tester at random, into which some of these metathesis forms had been mixed. His performance is recorded below, together with such erasures and comments as were of interest:

	Dictated Word	Correct Spelling[4]	Patient Wrote	Gloss
(9)	*ʾarnak*	**ʾrnq**	**ʾrnq**	'wallet'
(10)	*hištaper*	**hštpr**	**ht**, erased this and then correctly wrote **hštpr**	'improved'
(11)	*historiya*	**hysṭwryh**	**hysṭwryh**	'history'
(12)	*haštala*	**hštlh**	**hštlh**	'transplantation'
(13)	*tsisa*	**tsysh**	**tsysh**	'fermentation'
(14)	*hictaref*	**hṣṭrf**	see below	'joined'

When asked to write down the word /hictaref/, Dudu began by writing <ht> , while saying to himself [hic] (the correct form of the first syllable). He added, and then erased a <ṭ> , replaced it with a <ṣ> and then erased everything he had written. He began again with <hct> but erased this. Wrote <ṣrf> (the root form!) and put ht> before it. Finally, he gave up.

---

[3]There are two graphemes for /t/, "tav" represented here as <t> and "tet" which will be represented as <T> .

[4]<ʾ> represents "aleph"; <q> = "qof" = [k] ; <ṭ> = "tet" = [t] ; <ṣ> = "cade" = [c] ([ts]); <y> = "yod" (either /i/ or /y/); <f> = word-final "pe" = [f] ; other word-final letters have a dot over them; <w> = "vav" (either /v/, /u/ or /o/); ʿ = "ayin" [ʿ] .

	Dictated Word	Correct Spelling	Patient Wrote	Gloss
(15)	*holand*	**hwlnd**	**hwlnd**	'Holland'
(16)	*ša'on*	**š^{c}wn**	**š^{c}wn**	'watch'
(17)	*hatrada*	**hṭrdh**	**hṭrdh**	'nuisance'
(18)	*hit'amlut*	**ht^{c}mlwt**	**ht^{c}mlwt**	'gymnastics'
(19)	*hatsasa*	**htssh**	**htssh**	'fermentation'
(20)	*hictamek*	**hṣṭmq**	see below	

The word *hictamek* means 'it shrank'; *cimuk* is 'a raisin', i.e. a shrunken grape. Dudu said "I know what a *cimuk* is" and wrote this word down correctly <ṣmwq> . Then he said to himself [hicamek] (or ?[hitcamek]). He wrote <ht> , erased it, wrote <hṣmq> , and erased that, too. Now, he said "he" <h> then "tav" <t>. Here, the therapist intervened, as the patient was showing signs of frustration.

	Dictated Word	Correct Spelling	Patient Wrote	Gloss
(21)	*hitraxeš*	**htrxś**	**htršx** (incorrect metathesis; corrected it immediately)	'happened'
(22)	*hištaxrer*	**hštxrr**	**hštxrr** (the only metathesized form he got right the first time)	'freed himself'
(23)	*hišxir*	**hšxyr**	**ht** (perseveration); erased it and wrote word correctly	'blackened'
(24)	*mictaber*	**mṣṭbr**	see below	'accumulates'

In this case, the sudden change from the past tense to the present, with its initial /m/, and the two previous words, which both began with [hiš], caused Dudu to say to himself several times [hiš]. He did not write anything down and we stopped the dictation.

Words which did not involve metathesis were written down quickly and correctly. Of particular note are examples 11 and 12. Both have sibilant-dental stop sequences but neither belongs to the hitpa'el verb class, in which metathesis takes place. They caused no problem at all and were recorded immediately.

Some of the words dictated have metathesis involving the affricate /c/. Phonetically, this affricate may be regarded as [ts], but this cannot be the reason Dudu wrote [ht] in these cases for the following reasons: (i) there were many examples in his written compositions of failure to write the stop after the continuant stridents, too, e.g. * <mtšmš> for <mštmš> , i.e. [mištameš] 'he uses' (here and elsewhere an asterisk indicates the patient's deviant form); * <lhtšm^c> for <lhštm^c> , i.e. [lehištaméa] 'to hear from someone else'; * <htswbb> for <hstwbb> , i.e. [histovev] 'he turned around'; etc.; and (ii) he never elsewhere recorded <ṣ> as <ts> (note the word *cimuk* in connection with example (20)) nor, conversely, did he replace <ts> by <c> (note examples (13) and (19).

Subsequent to this dictation, which was given on June 19, 1974, his therapist taught or (as it is impossible to believe that he wrote the metathesized forms in this way before his impairment) retaught Dudu the correct spellings. He was not retaught what happens when the first stem consonant is the voiced dental sibilant /z/. In this case, there is not only metathesis but the /t/ agrees in voicing with the /z/, i.e. it is always pronounced as the dental stop /d/. In writing, the letter "dalet" <d> is used. In short, no /t/ or <t> occurs in the metathesis, graphemically or phonetically.

The following brief dictation was given on July 7, i.e. almost three weeks after the first one. All forms involve metathesis.

	Dictated Word	Correct Spelling	Patient Wrote	Gloss
(25)	*histaben*	**hstbṅ**	**hstbṅ**	'soaped himself'
(26)	*hizdarez*	**hzdrz**	**htzrz**	'acted diligently'
(27)	*hizdaqeq*	**hzdqq**	**htzqq**	'needed'
	(*zakuk* 'need')			

Dudu wrote <htzqq> even though the word had been dictated three times with a grossly exaggerated lengthening of the [z], viz. *hizzz . . .*

(28)	*hištadel*	**hštdl**	**hštdl**	'tried, endeavored'
(29)	*hizdamen*	**hzdmṅ**	**htzmṅ**	'chanced'
	(*zman* 'time')			
(30)	*hištameš*	**hštmš**	**hštmš**	'used'
(31)	*hizdanev*	**hzdnb**	**htznb**	'tailed off'
	(*zanav* 'tail')			

It is clear from the above dictation that Dudu had learned his spelling lesson well. More important for our purposes is, of course, his deviant spelling on this occasion. All the words given above were written down at near-normal speed (allowing for his right hemiplegia) without erasures or comments.[5]

When speaking, Dudu never failed to apply the metathesis rule. He never said *[hitsaper], *[hitsader], *[hitzarez], etc. The confusion arose only in writing.

3.2. Preposition-Article Contraction (PAC)

After the bound prepositions [be] 'in', [ke] 'like', 'as', and [le] 'to', the /h/ of the definite article [ha] 'the' is always deleted, in both speaking and writing.[6] The vowel of the definite article is

[5] Four days later, in a short dictation of sentences, the colloquial verb form [hizdangef] was dictated. This verb means 'he went for a stroll down Dizengoff Street' (a main thoroughfare in Tel-Aviv). The verb stem is lexically related to Dizengoff the name of the first mayor of the city. What Dudu wrote down for [hizdangef] was, in fact, <htdngf> (the <z> was omitted). Even though [hizdangef] is not so easily recognizable as a metathesized form, Dudu still indicated an "underlying" prefix /hit/.

[6] There are very few exceptions to this rule. They relate only to the non-deletion of the /h/ in certain proper nouns and adverbial phrases.

transferred to the bound preposition. Thus, <gn> [gan] 'a garden', <hgn> [hagan] 'the garden, <bgn> [began] 'in a garden' or <bgn> [bagan] 'in the garden'. But Dudu consistently wrote down *<bh...> , * < lh... > or * <kh...> , i.e. he failed to omit the <h> representing the definite article, although he did not insert incorrect graphemes anywhere else in his writing. The insertion of <h> in these cases is clearly conditioned by the underlying morphemic composition of the words, which we discuss in the following section. The <h> in these post-prepositional positions was always deleted in Dudu's speech.

4. THE MORPHOPHONEMIC REPRESENTATIONS AND THEORETICAL IMPLICATIONS

Most linguistic theories assume a level of representation deeper than the surface phonetic level. This deeper level is often referred to as "morphophonemic", "phonological", or "systematic phonemic". One of the functions of this level is to set out the strings of bound morphemes which make up a word. Each morpheme is represented by a single basic morpheme from which others are derived by rule. The Hebrew hitpa'el reflexive prefix surfaces phonetically as [hit], e.g. [hitkadem] 'he progressed', etc., as [hiSt], e.g. [histaken] 'he endangered himself', or as [hizd] in [hizdaken] 'he grew old', but it is clear that the "s" or the "z" (in [hist] or [hizd] respectively) are not part of the reflexive pronoun. They belong to the stem of the verb. The speaker knows that "hit" is in a sense basic and that if it precedes a verb stem with an initial strident consonant a rule of metathesis must apply. According to the theory, this knowledge is represented at the morphophonemic level by strings such as / hit + kadem /, / hit + sader /, / hit + zaken /, etc. (where + is an internal morpheme boundary), although the latter two strings are never realized as such either phonetically or graphemically. Psychological evidence in favour of such a theory is, by the nature of things, rare. It is, therefore, of especial interest to linguists that, under pathological conditions, abstract forms can and do emerge.

The morphophonemic analysis of such strings as [bagan] 'in the garden', [lakolnóa] 'to the cinema', etc. proceeds along similar lines. We have already seen that [ha] is the basic morpheme signifying the definite article. When following the prepositions / b / 'in', / l / 'to', or / k / 'as, like', the initial / h / of / ha / is deleted (by rule). Thus, the morphophonemic string for 'in the garden' would be / b + ha + gan /.[7] As in the case of metathesis, the / h / of the definite article never surfaces in this environment, either in speaking or in writing. Nevertheless, after brain damage, this abstract form did surface in this patient's writing.

Not all linguistic theories have, however, recognized a level deeper than the phonetic or accept the notion of a basic morpheme. In a theory recently outlined by Vennemann (1974), for example, there is only one (lexical) level of representation and that is the phonetic. Representations such as / hit + sader /, / hit + zaken /, / b + ha + gan / are not part of such a grammar and therefore there are no basic morphemes. Rather, redundancy rules will interpret the surface phonetic level of representation. The evidence from aphasia presented here, however, strongly supports the concept of a morphophonemic level.[8]

[7] Alternatively, with underlying / e / following the consonant representing the preposition. The point is immaterial, since the writing system does not indicate vowels.

[8] Dudu's spelling in these instances is a rather interesting example of what Hécaen wrote concerning the parietally damaged patient: "The main disorder may be considered as a disturbance in the programming of the graphic message, ... in the organization of code structures principally on the level of the morpheme, the control which provides the correspondence between phonic and graphic structures having disappeared" (1967:156).

5. THE SEMITIC ROOT AND VERB CLASS TRANSFER

Since the major area of breakdown to be discussed in this section concerns the verb, a brief outline of the Hebrew verbal system is needed.

There are seven Verb Classes (henceforth VCs), each of which is characterized by a different set of vowels and, sometimes, by specific prefixes. Each VC has three tenses: past, present and future. There is also an infinitival form and an imperative, both of which are formally similar to the future tense. The past and future tenses are inflected for three persons, two numbers (singular (s) and plural (p)), and two genders (masculine (m) and feminine (f)). The first person is common to both genders, but the second and third persons have different endings, depending on gender. The present tense is, however, characterized only by a gender and number distinction. The basic vowel patterns and prefixes are set out below. The forms given are the third person masculine singular (3ms) of the regular triconsonantal verb. In the first column, the traditional Hebrew name for the VC is given, accompanied by a number. We shall refer to the number throughout.

	Past	**Present**	**Future**
VC1 (Qal or pa'al)	C*a*C*a*C	C*o*C*e*C	*yi*CC*o*C / *yi*CC*a*C
VC2 (pi'el)	C*i*C*e*C	*me*C*a*C*e*C	*ye*C*a*C*e*C
VC3 (pu'al)	C*u*C*a*C	*me*C*u*C*a*C	*ye*C*u*C*a*C
VC4 (hitpa'el)	*hit*C*a*C*e*C	*mit*C*a*C*e*C	*yit*C*a*C*e*C
VC5 (hif'il)	*hi*CC*i*C	*ma*CC*i*C	*ya*CC*i*C
VC6 (huf'al)	*hu*CC*a*C	*mu*CC*a*C	*yu*CC*a*C
VC7 (nif'al)	*ni*CC*a*C	*ni*CC*a*C	*yi*C*a*C*e*C

There are syntactic-semantic relationships between the VCs. Thus, VC3 and VC6 are almost exclusively used as passive forms, generally of VC2 and VC5 respectively, whereas VC7 is not uncommonly the passive form corresponding to VC1. VC4 often denotes reflexivity, reciprocity or mutuality, whereas VC5 denotes causation or inchoativity. There are, however, many exceptions. In general, VC1 and VC2 are the basic classes functioning somewhat similarly to Indo-European conjugation systems. As in conjugation systems, given a certain root, we cannot predict phonologically whether the verb is to be assigned to VC1 or to VC2. (Unlike the Indo-European system, a root may occur in both VC1 and VC2 with generally unpredictable semantic differences). Furthermore, in addition to their primary functions, VC4, 5, and 7 may be used as "basic" verb classes, i.e. with no semantic-syntactic overtones. Examples are [histakel] (VC4) 'looked at', [hifgin] (VC5) 'demonstrated', [nixnas] (VC7) 'entered', etc.

Assuming that there are underlying roots for verbs, it is clear that we have to assign verb class markers indicating to which verb class or verb classes any one verb belongs. It also follows that a certain root may appear in only one VC or in all seven, though probably most verbs have forms in two or three different VCs.[9] One further point must be stressed, namely that verbs cannot be arbitrarily switched from one VC to another.

[9] For further discussion on the VC system, see Aronson (Berman) (1969), Ariel (1972).

We may illustrate the above points with three roots chosen at random:

$\sqrt{\overline{\text{šbr}}}$		
VC1	*šavar*	'he broke'
VC2	*šiber*	'he smashed'
VC3	*šubar*	'it was smashed' (passive of VC2)
VC4	*hištaber*	'it refracted'
VC5	non-occurring (henceforth N-O)	
VC6	N-O	
VC7	*nišbar*	'it was broken' (passive of VC1)

Note that this particular root has no VC5 **hišbir* or VC6 **hušbar*. The speaker would identify such possible, though non-occurring, forms as meaning 'cause to break', though they would never be used in normal speech.

$\sqrt{\overline{\text{gmr}}}$	'finish'	
VC1	*gamar*	'he finished'
VC7	*nigmar*	'it was finished'
VC2-6	N-O	
$\sqrt{\overline{\text{tkn}}}$	'repair'	
VC1	N-O	
VC2	*tiken*	'he repaired'
VC3	*tukan*	'it was repaired'
VC4	N-O	
VC5	*hitkin*	'he installed'
VC6	*hutkan*	'it was installed'
VC7	N-O	

Turning now to Dudu, we note that he sometimes transferred verbs from one class to another. All the examples given in Chart A, with one exception, occurred during free conversation. They were nearly always spoken without hesitation on Dudu's part and he never corrected the mistakes, unless they were pointed out to him. Practically all the errors were made during the period mid-January to March 1, 1974.

As regards column 6 of Chart A, the following should be noted:

a) Those verbs marked M(N-O) indicate that a lexical gap has been filled. The patient rendered the verb in a VC which has no realization in non-pathological speech, for the particular verb in question.

b) Those verbs marked M and/or S, where S indicates a syntactic deviation, are ambiguous as far as interpretation of the deviation is concerned. One could claim that Dudu was aware of the correct syntactic process but erred at the morphological level. Consider example (xvii), where the patient used *yišavru* instead of *yišberu*. The deviant sentence he uttered was:

*1. *hem yišavru et haxalonot* (*et* is an object marker (OM))
  *'they will be broken the windows.'

CHART A

	1	2		3	4	5	6
	Correct form	Grammatical analysis		Gloss	Deviant form	Grammatical analysis (of #4)	Possible interpre-tation
i)	*levate*	VC2	Inf.	'to pronounce'	*livto*	VC1	M (N-O)
ii)	*šalax*	VC1	3 msg. past	'he sent'	*šileax*	VC2 (archaic)	M (N-O)
iii)	*yisog*	VC7	3 msg. fut.	'he will retreat'	*yasug*	VC1	M (N-O)
	(The canonic form *ya*+C*u*C is typical of VC1 future forms in biconsonantal roots)						
iv)	*gazaz*	VC1	3 msg. past	'he cut'	*gizez*	VC2	M (N-O)
v)	*nifgeʾa*	VC7	3 fsg.	'she was hurt'	*hitpagʾa*	VC4	M (N-O)
vi)	*kibsa*	VC2	3 fsg. past	'she laundered'	*hixvisa*	VC5	M (N-O)
vii)	*yatkinu*	VC7	3 mpl. fut.	'they will install'	*yitkenu*	VC1	M (N-O)
viii)	*tibahalu*	VC7	2 mpl. fut.	'you will be shocked'	*tivhalu*	VC1	M (N-O)
ix)	*higati*	VC5	1 msg. past	'I arrived'	*hagati*	VC1	M (N-O)
	(Alternative explanation: Phonemic paraphasia /a/ for /i/ with incorrect regressive assimilation)						
x)	*niv(h)elet*	VC7	3 fsg. pres.	'she is shocked'	*mitnavelet*	VC4	M (N-O)
xi)	*henaxti*	VC5	1 msg. past	'I placed'	*manaxti*	VC1	M
xii)	*yefutru*	VC3	3 mpl.	'they will be dismissed'	*yipatru*	VC7	M
xiii)	*yamutu*	VC1	3 mpl. fut.	'they will die'	*yamitu*	VC5 (transitive)	M or S
	(Alternatively, with phonemic paraphasia /i/ for /u/)						
xiv)	*lehistaxsex*	VC4	Inf. (Int.)	'to squabble'	*lesaxsex*	VC2 (transitive)	M or S
xv)	*higdilu*	VC5	3 mpl. past (trans.)	'they enlarged'	*gadlu*	VC1 (int.)	M or S
xvi)	*mekalkel*	VC2	3 msg. pres. (trans.)	'spoil'	*mitkalkel*	VC4 (int.)	M or S
xvii)	*yišberu*	VC1	3 mpl. fut. (active)	'they will break'	*yišavru*	VC7 (pass.)	M or S
xviii)	*tipagʾi*	VC7	2 fsg. fut. (pass.)	'you will be hurt'	*tifga*	VC1 (active)	M or S

The correct form is:

2. *hem yišberu et haxalonot*
 'they will break the windows'

One can claim that Dudu confused the active-passive relationship at the syntactic level, or that he was quite aware of the distinction–intended the active form– but assigned the verb to the wrong VC.[10] The same ambiguity of interpretation exists with regard to transitive-intransitive relations.[11]

The following general observations must be noted:

i) ALL deviations may be accounted for at the morphological level. Basically, Dudu erred in the assignment of verbs to the correct VC.
ii) Dudu never inserted an arbitrary set of vowels into the verb root; he employed the rules which spell out the grammatical, i.e. vocalic, elements within the root.
iii) The verbs set out in Chart A are all in daily use. Many are quite frequent.[12]

Before discussing the theoretical implications of the data, it is necessary to emphasize a point of considerable importance: Dudu never made similar errors in categories other than the verb. Prima facie, there is no morphological reason why he should not have done so. In the noun system, just as in the verb, there is often an identifiable root, accompanied by differing affixes and internal vowel patterns. For example, non-verbal forms related to the root $\sqrt{\text{šbr}}$ 'break' (see above) are:

šavir	'fragile'
šever	'fracture'
mašber	'crisis; breaking-point' (where *ma-* is a nominal prefix)
šover (mayim)	'break(water)'
švira	'breaking' (nominalized form of VC1)
etc.	

Dudu did not make errors such as saying *mašber* when he intended *šever*. Nor did he exploit lexical gaps in the noun system, as he did on occasion in the verbal system. At first sight, it might appear that the essential distinction between the verb and noun systems is that the former can be described in terms of a restricted number of classes–seven–whereas a similar classification of nouns would be arbitrary and require an excessive number of classes, since there are so many possible vowel patterns and affix combinations available. There are, however, noun forms which are directly related to VC's and yet even they were never impaired. We refer, in particular, to nominalized forms.[13]

Some VCs have associated with them a nominalized form, which may indicate either an action or a derived nominal. Thus, VC1 has the pattern /CCiC + a/, VC2 /CiCuC/, VC5 /ha + CCaC + a/, etc. For example, [bdika] (VC1) indicates either '(the) examining (of somebody)' or the examination itself;

[10] Independent testing indicates the latter explanation as being more likely. Exercises based on active/passive transformations were generally performed without error.

[11] The active/passive and transitive/intransitive (or causative/non-causative) relations are among the most prominent semantic-syntactic aspects of the VC system.

[12] There are no dependable frequency tables for spoken Hebrew. Our remarks on frequency must be taken as being impressionistic.

[13] Agentive nouns are also closely related to VC's. Thus, barring obvious semantic constraints, the present tense form of a verb can be used, e.g. [šomer] (VC1) 'a guard', [megadel] (VC2) 'a grower, [malxin] (VC5) 'a composer', etc. No VC transfer ever took place in Dudu's speech in instances such as these.

[hazmana (VC5) '(the) inviting (of somebody)' or the invitation itself. (This is a gross oversimplification of a relationship replete with idiosyncrasies on the semantic-syntactic level (see Aronson (Berman) (1973)), as well as at the morphological level). Sometimes the nominal form is assigned to a VC other than that of the related verb. For example, [kvisa], '(the) washing (of something), laundry' is a nominal form of VC1, whereas the verbal forms are assigned to VC2. In other cases, the nominalized form is unpredictably absent in one, or both, of its principal syntactic functions, e.g. *[gmira] 'the finishing of' does not exist, even though there is a VC1 form [gamar] 'he finished'.

The association between the verb and the nominal was clearly illustrated by Dudu on a few occasions. Note the following three examples (spontaneous conversation):

1a. Intended Sentence

haiša	*kibsa*	*et*	*habgadim*
'the woman	washed	(OM)	the clothes'

1b. Dudu's Utterance

haiša (then three times to himself, *hakvisa*, the nominalized form of *kibsa*) *xibsa* [sic] *et habgadim*

2a. Intended Sentence

hacayar	*hitbayeš*	*laxtom* ...
'the painter	was ashamed	to sign ...'

2b. Dudu's Utterance

hacayar	*buša,*[14]	*lo,*	(pause)	*hitbayeš* ...
'the painter	shame,	no,	(pause)	was ashamed ...'

3a. Intended Sentence

axare	*še-nifcati* ...
'after	(that) I was wounded ...'

3b. Dudu's Utterance

axare	*še* ...	*še* ...	*axare*	*hapci'a*	*šeli*
'after	that ...	that ...	after	the wound	mine (= my being wounded)'

The morpheme /še/ as in the last example requires a finite verb form after it. Instead of supplying such a form, Dudu backtracked, deleted /še/ and then correctly used a nominalized form after the preposition.

[14] A biconsonantal root, with a VC1 nominalized form of C*u*C + *a*.

Examples of this type indicate further the problems the patient was having with verbal forms. They show, moreover, that the related nominal form was clearly accessible to him.[15]

The data discussed in this section strongly support the concept of the morpheme. Of particular interest, however, (since one may object that this is a concept that hardly needs support!), is the way words disintegrated. The grammatical morphemes, i.e. the vowels which denote tense, aspect, etc., in the verb, were replaced by another set of vowels. The consonantal framework,[16] representing the verbal root, remained stable, thus supporting the notion of morphemes consisting entirely of consonants–an abstract notion, since these morphemes are unpronounceable. Furthermore, the need for morphological markers or features, such as the VC markers, is supported. The simplest and most direct explanation of Dudu's impairment is that he could not retrieve these VC markers, although the consonantal root and the rules which spell out the shape of the grammatical morphemes were available to him.

The difference in Dudu's performance with verbs from that with non-verbs might reflect a difference in lexical storage, the former being root-derived, the latter fully specified in the lexicon. The idea of such a dichotomy has some independent linguistic support. We point out some of the factors which must be considered:

(a) The number of different vowel patterns required in verbs is very restricted and can be controlled by morphological markers. This obviates the necessity of deciding which vowel pattern is basic within a VC. Any attempt to set up one underlying representation is without motivation and can only lead to ad hoc adjustments. The noun system, however, is not so restricted. A large array of unpredictable vowel patterns (with or without accompanying prefixes or suffixes) is found in Hebrew morphology.

(b) If verbs are lexicalized in consonantal root form, we can make the generalization that if a root has four consonants then it must be assigned to VC2. These are some 200 verbs of this type. Interestingly enough, this generalization was never violated by Dudu. No parallel generalization can be made for non-verbs.

(c) Co-occurrence restrictions appear to hold for verbs (unless borrowed or derived from nouns). Thus, two liquids cannot be adjacent (**rl*, **lr*), a pair of obstruents differing only in voicing is not found (**td*, **dt*, **kg*, **gk*), the first two consonants in the root cannot be identical, etc. These co-occurrence restrictions do not apply to nouns. The role of the vowels in such constraints is nil (Barkai, 1978).

(d) Foreign verbs are adapted to the vowel system of Hebrew, e.g. English 'bluff', Hebrew *bilef*; English 'modernize', Hebrew *midren* (see also fn. 5). Nouns are not adapted but retain forms close to the original, allowing for the usual phonological adaptation. Thus, the corresponding noun forms for the above are *blof* 'bluff' and *modernizacya* 'modernization'.

---

[15] For further evidence from aphasia concerning nominalizations, see Whitaker (1972).

[16] Another type of error relating to morpheme structure and to the verbal system was an incorrect distribution of affixes. Thus *[macbiti] where *ma-* is a present tense morpheme (VC5) but the *-ti* suffix is a past tense morpheme; *[nociu] where the initial /n/ stands for the 1st person plural but the final /u/ is a suffix indicating the 2nd or 3rd person plural. Another interpretation of *[manaxti] parallels the analysis of deviant *[macbiti]. The form *[mitnavelet] may be based on a wrong analysis of surface [niv(h)al] where *ni* represents the VC7 prefix. Dudu may have regarded the root as containing the three consonants n, v and l and then wrongly assigned it to VC4. This, together with a possible wrong analysis of *[manaxti] as being derived from a root m-n-x, would be examples of root reconstruction by him.

The above, together with the evidence from Dudu, are strong arguments supporting the notion that verbs are stored according to roots, with associated VC markers, whereas nouns are spelt out in full, i.e. with vowel specifications. The consequences of the above claims should have repercussions for most current lexical theories (see, for example, Halle (1973), Vennemann (1974), Hooper (1975), Lightner (1975), Jackendoff (1975)).

The difficulty Dudu had in retrieving VC markers sheds considerable light on a controversial problem in Hebrew, namely spirantization. This is an area in which he also suffered impairment and to which we now turn our attention.

6. SPIRANTIZATION

In the previous section, we have shown that Dudu had morphological impairment which, to a large extent, affected his ability to retrieve certain morphological features. On the other hand, when appraising his overall performance, there is no evidence whatsoever that he suffered any impairment to the phonological component. Let us assume a process in which there is impairment–and spirantization is such a process–and that on purely linguistic grounds there is doubt whether it should be described morphologically or phonologically. In such a case, it is clear that the performance of an aphasic patient may take us a considerable way towards deciding the issue. Clearly, one would link the breakdown in spirantization with the previously established breakdown in morphology, rather than claim that the two have no relationship at all and that the breakdown in spirantization is the only case of impairment in the phonological component. Moreover, the descriptive analysis employed by the linguist comes into focus. That is to say, what kind of rules or constraints (or the lack of them) does a linguist use to decide whether a certain phenomenon should be regarded as morphological or phonological? Clearly, if, as in this case, it can be shown that spirantization is a morphological process, and not a phonological one, then the kinds of arguments used by a linguist supporting the latter approach are refuted from a language particular point of view and challenged on language general grounds.

6.1 The Distribution

Hebrew has six stops / p t k b d g /, of which / p b / and some[17] of the / k / alternate with their corresponding spirants / f v / and / x / respectively. The enviroment in which these alternations take place will be discussed at length in 6.2 below.

The stop/fricative distribution may be illustrated by the following chart based on the Hebrew verbal system. Although these alternations are also found in categories other than the verb, their frequency there–both textual and lexical–is somewhat more limited. Furthermore, most of the errors made by Dudu involved verbs. In the chart below, P represents any alternating stop and F any alternating spirant.

[17] Note rule P4, in 6.2.1.

	Past	Present	Future
VC1	PaFaF	PoFeF	*yi* + FPoF[18]
VC2	PiPeF	*me* + FaPeF	*ye* + FaPeF
VC3	PuPaF	*me* + FuPaF	*ye* + FuPaF
VC4	*hit* + PaPeF	*mit* + PaPeF	*yit* + PaPeF
VC5	*hi* + FP*i*F	*ma* + FP*i*F	*ya* + FP*i*f
VC6	*hu* + FPaF	*mu* + FPaF	*yu* + FPaF
VC7	*ni* + FPaF[18]	*ni* + FPaF[18]	*yi* + PaFeF

The above chart may be illustrated with the root *kpr* 'atone'. Some of the VC's do not exist for this root but have been filled in.

	Past	Present	Future
VC1	*kafar*	*kofer*	*yixpor*
VC2	*kiper*	*mexaper*	*yexaper*
VC3	*kupar*	*mexupar*	*yexupar*
VC4	*hitkaper*	*mitkaper*	*yitkaper*
VC5	*hixpir*	*maxpir*	*yaxpir*
VC6	*huxpar*	*muxpar*	*yuxpar*
VC7	*nixpar*	*nixpar*	*yikafer*

6.2 The Approaches

Two conflicting grammars have been proposed to account for these alternations. One approach we shall call the "phonological" or P-approach, the other the "morphological" or M-approach. The main points of both hypotheses are given below. They will be followed by a description of the patient's deviations (Chart B).

[18] In many lexical items, there is an ongoing change such that *yi*FPoF → *yi*FFoF, e.g. *yitpos* → *yitfos* 'he will catch', *yidpok* (rare) → *yidfok* 'he will knock (fuck)', etc. Likewise, in VC7, *ni*FpaF → *ni*FFaF, e.g. *nitpas* → *nitfas* 'it was caught', *nidpak* (?) → *nidfak* 'he was fucked up'.

6.2.1 The P-approach

P1. In VC2, 3, and 4, R_2[19] is geminated [+G].[20]

P2. A vowel is deleted before a single consonant followed by a suffix consisting of a single vowel. This rule does not directly refer to the spirantization process except as regards ordering. Its reflex can be seen in several of the examples in the patient's data.

P4. Those / k /'s which do not alternate are derived from an underlying voiceless uvular stop / q /. By rule P4, / q / is specified as [k] in all environments (see Chomsky and Halle 1968:170, fn. 7).

P5. All [+G] segments must be degeminated.

The above rules may be summarized as follows:

P1. $R_2 \rightarrow$ [+G] in VC2, 3, 4

P2. [p, b, k] [f, v, x] /V______
-G

P3. $V \rightarrow \emptyset / \_\_\_ C + V$

P4. $q \rightarrow k$

P5. [+G] $\rightarrow$ [-G]

The following crucial ordering of rules applies:

P1 must be ordered before P2, P4 and P5

P2 must be ordered before P3

Employing three examples with which the patient made mistakes, the above rules may be illustrated with some sample derivations:

(i) [kibsa] VC2; 3fs past 'she laundered'

Morphophonemic representation: / kibes + a /

P1: *kibes + a*
[+G]

P2: non-applicable as / k / is not post-vocalic and / b / is [+G].

P3: *kibs + a*
[+G]

P4: non-applicable

P5: *kibs + a*

Phonetic output: [kibsa].

Stress is ignored throughout as it is irrelevant to this discussion.

(ii) [šavar] VC1; 3ms past 'he broke'

Morphophonemic representation: / šabar /

P2: (only rule applicable) *šavar*

Phonetic output: [šavar]

---

[19]The three radical consonants in the verbal root will be referred to as R_1, R_2 and R_3 respectively.

[20]Gemination is motivated (i) on the basis of alternations such as [lev] 'heart' ~ [libi] 'my heart', [levavot] 'hearts'; (ii) by the fact that all quadriliteral verbs are assigned to VC2, 3, or 4; (iii) by the failure of vowel truncation to apply before [+G] in certain nouns (contrast [davar] – [dvarim] 'thing – things' with [sabal] – [sabalim] 'porter – porters') correlating with the fact that VT never applies before a consonant cluster; (iv) by the failure of spirantization post-vocalically in certain cases; (v) by its phonetic realization in highly formal, literary renderings of poetry, the Bible, etc. In this last case, there is no problem of absolute neutralization. Nevertheless, phonetic gemination is so highly restricted that many speakers are probably unaware of its existence. For a fuller discussion, see Chomsky (1951), Chayen (1968), Ornan (1972), Barkai (1972), Schwarzwald (1973). Although concerned with Biblical Hebrew, Sampson (1973) and Barkai (1974) are also relevant.

(iii) [xošvim] VC1; 3mp present 'they think'

Morphophonemic representation: / xošeb + im /

P1: non applicable

P2: *xošev + im*

P3: *xošv + im*

P4, 5: non-applicable

Phonetic output: [xošvim]

The above P-approach is representative of much of the work done on Hebrew within the framework of Transformational Generative Phonology. It must be stressed that these rules have been posited on independent linguistic grounds by many of the linguists referred to previously (vide fn. 20).

6.2.2 The M-approach

This incorporates two principles:

(i) Absolute neutralization, whereby an underlying distinction which is not realized phonetically but is totally merged with other segments, is forbidden (see Kiparsky (1968)). This does not permit rules such as P4 and P5 or, by implication, an underlying / q / and rule P1.

(ii) The "alternation condition", which prevents a rule from applying to non-alternating parts of morphemes (Kiparsky 1968). Adherence to this condition rules out, for example, the possibility of positing an underlying bi-labial stop in R_3 position, since this part of the verb never shows alternation, i.e. a R_3 labial obstruent is always realized as a labio-dental fricative.

The M-approach, as its name suggests, regards the realization of the relevant obstruents as being controlled, to a large extent, by morphological features.

The status of the five phonological rules can now be considered from the viewpoint of the M-approach:

P1. This rule is rejected, as it requires the introduction of a phonetically determined feature, i.e. gemination, which is not realized phonetically.

P2. This rule will be replaced by a lexical statement as to the distribution of the stop : fricative alternations in terms of VC's. The post-vocalic environment is rejected.

P3. The rule may stand. However, there is no need for ordering it after the spirantization rule. The main purpose for ordering it after P2 was to spirantize the stops post-vocalically. Since the morphological approach does not recognize any such environment, and since it has underlying / f v x / in R_3 position, the ordering is irrelevant. The remarks made on the alternation condition (ii) above/ will be recalled.

P4. The rule is rejected, as it is a rule of absolute neutralization. In its place, the M-approach will assign a marker to the / k / stating whether it undergoes spirantization or not, depending on the lexical item involved (note Barkai (1972)).

P5. This rule is also rejected, since it involves absolute neutralization. We can now sum up the M-approach, as follows:

M1. Spirantization is a morphologically determined phenomenon and has no purely phonetic environment.

M2 = P3

Elsewhere, lexical features will state whether the / k / can, or cannot, be spirantized.

In short, the P-approach makes use of phonetically determined features, even though they are not always realized at the phonetic level. Further, it employs rule ordering. The M-approach makes greater use of morphological features and does not require rule ordering.

6.2.3 The data

The mistakes set out in Chart B were recorded during six sessions, between mid-January 1974 and March 1, 1974. At this point work with the patient was interrupted but further interviews between mid-April and mid-July revealed no errors in spirantization, indicating that the patient had remastered the correct distribution of these obstruents. Unless otherwise stated, all errors were made in spontaneous conversation.

CHART B

	Correct form	Grammatical analysis		Gloss	Deviant rendering	Type of substitution
	Verbs					
i)	*kibsa*	VC2	3 fsg. past	'she laundered'	*xibsa*[21]	/ x / for / k /
ii)	*xošvim*	VC1	mpl. pres.	'(they) think'	*košvim*	/ k / for / x /
	(The only example of substitution of a non-alternating / x /, historically dervied from a voiceless pharyngeal fricative.)					
iii)	*kiblu*	VC2	3 mpl. past	'(they) received'	*xiblu*	/ x / for / k /
	(The above error made in reading, even though non-alternating / k / and / x / have different graphemes. The initial / k / is non-alternating and would be derived from / q / in the "phonological" approach. All other / k /'s mentioned in this chart which are substituted by / x / are alternating / k /'s.)					
iv)	*kisa*	VC2	3 msg. past	'he covered'	*xisa*[21]	/ x / for / k /

[21] The "incorrect" forms in (i), (iv) and possibly (v) are found in sub-standard non-pathological speech. However, Dudu's later improved speech did not indicate any of these deviations and they are probably to be associated with his aphasic condition, though we cannot be too certain of this point. In case (v), he was citing the fifth commandment, where the opening word is / kabed / 'honour'. It is not likely he would make a sub-standard error while citing a formal text.

v)	*kabed*	VC2	2 msg. imp.	'honor!'	*xabed*[21]	/ x / for / k /
vi)	*lixtov*	VC1	inf.	'to write'	*liktov*	/ k / for / x /
vii)	*kibsa*	VC2	3 fsg. past	'she laundered'	*kivsa*	/ v / for / b /

(Note example (i). These two variants were uttered on different dates.)

viii)	*kavaš*	VC1	3 msg. past	'he conquered'	*kabaš*	/ b / for / v /
ix)	*koveš*	VC1	3 msg. pres.	'he conquers'	*kobeš*	/ b / for / v /

(Examples (viii) and (ix) were uttered within a few minutes of each other. However, within the same short period of time, he also used correct variants [kavšu] 'they conquered' and [lixboš] 'to conquer'.]

x)	*nupcu*	VC3	3 mpl. past	'(they) were shattered'	*nufcu*	/ f / for / p /
xi)	*nipcu*	VC2	3 mpl. past	'(they) shattered'	*nifcu*	/ f / for / p /

(Examples (x) and (xi) uttered on different occasions.)

xii)	*yefater*	VC2	3 msg. fut.	'he will sack'	*yepater*	/ p / for / f /

(This example could be regarded not as an error in spirantization, but as one of VC transfer. Dudu's output [yepater] is very similar to [yipater], with a stop in R_1 position, which is the VC7 future form.)

xiii)	*šavar*	VC1	3 msg. past	'he broke'	*šabar*	/ b / for / v /

Nouns

xiv)	*avixa*	'your father'	*abixa*	/ b / for / v /

(Possibly confused with [aba] 'daddy'.)

xv)	*bekoma*	'on (=*be*-) floor'	*bexoma*	/ x / for (non-alternating) / k /

(After the tree proclitic prepositions / be /, / ke / and / le /, spirantization may take place, although this rule has generally died out of colloquial Hebrew. The replacement of / x / for non-alternating / k / is, of course, deviant.)

xvi)	*hava'ad*	'the (*ha*-) committee'	*haba'ad*	/ v / for / b /

(After the definite article (*ha*-), the stop is used. However in this example, / v / is non-alternating, i.e. historically derived from / w / and is, therefore, deviant.)

6.2.4 The superiority of the M-approach

In the opening paragraph of this section (6), we stated why spirantization should be treated morphologically. Nevertheless, the two approaches and the data having been presented, the main arguments supporting the M-approach can now be given again, more forcefully:

1) The VC transfers discussed in detail in Section 5 were clearly MORPHOLOGICAL in nature, arising, as we have seen, from difficulty in retrieving the correct VC feature. Since the morphological analysis of spirantization also makes reference to VCs in accounting for the alternations (at least as far as verbs are concerned, where, indeed, most of the errors were made), we now have a UNITARY explanation for superficially different phenomena.

2) Dudu never made errors in any way involving factors which are indisputably phonological (or phonetic) in nature. In short, phonological rules, phonotactic statements, etc. were unimpaired. Phonological rules include those which are morphologically conditioned. Thus, in speaking,[22] Dudu never erred in metathesis (see Section 3a) although this rule is restricted to VC4. More directly related to our discussion on spirantization are the environments in which Dudu *never* made bilabial obstruent switches:

(i) in word-initial position;
(ii) in the environment #C____ ;
(iii) in word-final position;
(iv) in the environment V + ____ (in verbs);
(v) in R_3 position.

Points (i) to (iii) are covered by phonotactic statements. In (i), only / p / and never / f / occurs in word-final position (/ v /, derived historically from / w /, is found in this environment, though its function and lexical load are quite low). In (ii) and (iii), only the fricatives / f / and / v / occur, never, in native Hebrew words, their plosive counterparts. As regards point (iv), we may note that, with the exception of the future tense of VC7 (note comment after form (xii) in Chart B) as well as some other instances which are not relevant here, only the fricative variants are found in post-vocalic environment where the vowel is part of the prefix or, in other words, where the vowel is marked off from R_1 by the presence of a morpheme boundary. In Barkai (1975), arguments were presented from evidence based on dialect variations and children's speech, showing the need for a morphologically conditioned PHONOLOGICAL rule which allows spirantization in this one restricted environment. The further evidence from Dudu's performance supports these arguments.

Concerning point (v), we note that in R_3 position only / f / or / v / are to be found. The absence of any error is easily explained in terms of a theory which incorporates the alternation condition. There being no alternation of the labial obstruents in R_3 position, the alternation condition requires that the underlying representation of [f] and [v] be / f / and / v / (not / p / and / b /) respectively. Thus, the lack of alternation in this environment was as transparent to Dudu as the lack of alternation in, for example, the dental obstruents. The P-approach, on the other hand, cannot allow us any plausible explanation, since it requires the derivation of the fricatives from the stops by means of P2 which, we have noted in the cases of R_1 and R_2, is subject to error. Furthermore, deviations in word-initial velar obstruents cannot easily be explained in the light of the independently proposed rules since there is no post-

[22] The contrast between Dudu's writing, where he showed mistakes in metathesis, and his correct oral performance can be attributed to the different neurological factors which come into play in speech and writing.

vocalic phonological environment in which spirantization supposedly takes place. An explanation for this phenomenon in terms of the M-approach would claim that Dudu had difficulty in retrieving the rule features which govern the distribution of the voiceless velar obstruents. Rule features are similar to morphological features inasmuch as they are stated in the lexicon and are arbitrary in nature.

Finally, it must be stressed that Dudu never erred in substitutions of the continuancy value of the non-alternating obstruents. The phoneme pairs /t/ and /s/, /d/ and /z/, and /g/ and /g̲/ were never interchanged. In other words, we are dealing with morphophonemic paraphasia, rather than phonemic paraphasia. The latter is a well-known concept in aphasia, the former is not. Further research will reveal whether morphophonemic paraphasia is as rare as aphasic studies, in ignoring its existence, imply.

It would be presumptuous to claim that, since the P-approach fails so miserably to offer an explanation for Dudu's performance, all it entails, e.g. rule ordering, rules of absolute neutralization, etc., must be rejected out of hand. Nevertheless, we may cautiously surmise that, if linguistic theory, as embodied in Transformational Generative Phonology and exemplified in the P-approach, had been properly constrained, then the question whether a certain process is to be treated one way or another would not have arisen at all. The incorporation of constraints disallowing rule ordering, absolute neutralization, etc., as indeed has been proposed in Natural Generative Phonology (Vennemann (1971), Hooper (1973)), would have led us to a more insightful solution to this problem.

7. NEUROLOGICAL FACTORS

Within the aphasic paradigm, there is a hypothesis of a neurological nature which, though highly tentative and in need of further research, should be mentioned.

Whitaker (1971:110-111) discusses three patients who had a marked tendency towards nominalizing verbs. This preference for nominalization is, of course, reminiscent of Dudu's performance (note in particular p. 175). What all these patients had in common were lesions in the parietal lobe. One other patient had the reverse tendency: to convert nominals into their verbal or adjectival base forms. This patient had suffered damage to the frontal region. While such sparse evidence is insufficient for one to decide what, precisely, the correlation is between the site of the damage and a possible noun/verb distinction, the implications for some of the hypotheses raised in this article are obvious.

In other ways, too, of course, the possible separation of nouns from verbs in the brain could have important repercussions on linguistic theory at almost all levels, except, presumably, the phonetic. In view of our present state of ignorance on this point, it does not seem worthwhile speculating on this fascinating hypothesis.

The data discussed in this article may be related to an aphasic case, described variously by Schnitzer (1972) and Kehoe and Whitaker (1973). We refer especially to the latter article. The patient suffered lesions, in particular in the region of the supramarginal gyrus and in four smaller areas above it, all within the left parietal lobe. The patient experienced, inter alia, difficulty in nominalizing verbs and in deriving verbs from nouns; errors in the placement of idiosyncratic features within the lexicon, with resultant deviations such as 'satisfacation' and 'relaktion' for 'satisfaction' and 'relaxation' respectively. The possibility of the parietal region being some kind of control center for the retrieval of idiosyncratic morphological or exception features must be raised. Needless to say, much further research (in which, hopefully, linguists will co-operate!) is required before one can draw any conclusions.

8. CONCLUSIONS

We have presented aphasic evidence for the psychological reality of morphophonemic representations exemplified by spellings of morphemes in their underlying organization (metathesis and PAC). We have further brought evidence from the patient's oral performance showing how the word can be decomposed at the morphemic level, even when the morphemic material is embedded in the word and is discontinuous in nature. The data are highly suggestive of the psychological reality of the Semitic root which was, in general, easily retrieved by the patient, whereas the correct VC assignment of the root in question was not so easy. The patient's impairment as regards the morphology of the verb contrasted with the absence of any such impairment with regard to the noun. The contrast may well reflect a grammar which regards verbs as derived from roots, inter alia by means of vowel intercalation rules and nouns as being specified in the lexicon with full vocalic specification. However, the possibility of a neurophysiological distinction between noun and verb must be investigated further.

As far as spirantization is concerned, we claimed that a model such as Natural Generative Phonology, which does not allow absolute neutralization, incorporates the alternation condition and does not permit extrinsic ordering of morphophonemic rules, affords a much more insightful explanation of Dudu's deficit in terms of morphology rather than phonology. This conclusion was supported by the fact that elsewhere the patient had impairments which were clearly morphological in nature and, furthermore, by the fact that no Surface Phonetic Constraints or phonological rules were violated by Dudu.

In the light of the above discussion, it need hardly be stressed how important and valuable a tool the aphasic paradigm is for linguistic research. The damaged brain can tell us much about the organization of grammars, their different levels, rules, units, categories, etc. If it is true that "any interesting generative grammar will be dealing ... with mental processes" (Chomsky 1965:8), then it is rather amazing that, at least until recently, so little attention had been paid by linguists to neurolinguistic research. It is hoped that the future will bring a radical change to this rather sad situation. Such a change will, no doubt, reveal more about the mysteries of the human brain in general and about the nature of language in particular.

REFERENCES

ARIEL, S. 1972. "The functions of the conjugations in colloquial Israeli Hebrew." *BSOAS* 35:514-530.

ARONSON (Berman), R. 1969. "The predictability of vowel patterns in the Hebrew verb." *Glossa* 3(2):127-145.

__________. 1973. "*Hašemot hapo?olijim b?ivrit haxadaša* [=Verbal nouns in modern Hebrew]." Doctoral dissertation, Hebrew University, Jerusalem.

BARKAI, M. 1972. "Problems in the phonology of Israeli Hebrew." Doctoral dissertation, University of Illinois.

__________. 1974. "On duration and spirantization in Biblical Hebrew." *Linguistic Inquiry* 5:456-459.

__________. 1975. "On phonological representations, rules and opacity." *Lingua* 37:363-376.

__________. 1978. "Theoretical implications of consonant sequence constraints in Israeli Hebrew." *Afroasiatic Linguistics* 6(1):1-13.

CHAYEN, M. 1968. "An investigation of the phonology of modern Hebrew." Doctoral dissertation, University of London.

CHOMSKY, N. 1951. "The morphophonemics of modern Hebrew." M.A. thesis, University of Pennsylvania.

__________. 1965. *Aspects of the Theory of Syntax.* Cambridge, Mass.: MIT Press.

__________ and M. Halle. 1968. *The Sound Pattern of English.* New York: Harper & Row.

HALLE, M. 1973. "Prolegomena to a theory of word formation." *Linguistic Inquiry*, 4:3-16.

HECAEN, H. 1967. "Brain mechanisms suggested by studies of parietal lobes." In C.H.Millikan and F.L.Darley (eds.), *Brain Mechanisms Underlying Speech and Language*, pp.146-166. New York: Grune & Stratton.

HOOPER, J. 1973. "Aspects of natural generative phonology." Doctoral dissertation, University of California, Los Angeles.

__________. 1975. "The archi-segment in natural generative phonology." *Language* 51:536-560.

JACKENDOFF, R. 1975. "Morphological and semantic regularities in generative grammar." *Language* 51:639-671.

KEHOE, W.J. and H.A.Whitaker. 1973. "Lexical structure disruption in aphasia: a case study." In H. Goodglass and S. Blumstein (eds.), *Psycholinguistics and Aphasia*, pp.267-282. Baltimore: Johns Hopkins•University Press.

KIPARSKY, P. 1968. "How abstract is phonology?" In O. Fujimura (ed.), *Three dimensions of linguistic theory*, pp.5-56. Tokyo Institute for Advanced Studies of Language.

LIGHTNER, T.M. 1975. "The role of derivational morphology in generative grammar." *Language* 51:617-638.

ORNAN, U. 1972. "Ordered rules and the so-called phonologization of ancient allophones in Israeli Hebrew." Paper delivered at the International Conference of Linguistics, Bologna, Italy.

SAMPSON. G. 1973. "Duration in Hebrew consonants." *Linguistic Inquiry* 4:101-104.

SCHNITZER, M.L. 1972. *Generative Phonology–Evidence from Aphasia.* Pennsylvania State University Studies no. 34, Pennsylvania State University Park, Penn.

_______________. 1974. "Aphasiological evidence for five linguistic hypotheses." *Language* 50:300-315.

SCHWARZWALD, O. 1973. "Lexical representations, phonological processes and morphological patterns in Hebrew." Doctoral dissertation, University of Texas, Austin.

VENNEMANN, T. 1971. "Natural generative phonology." Paper delivered at annual meeting of the Linguistic Society of America, St. Louis, Missouri.

_______________. 1974. "Words and syllables in natural generative grammar." In *Papers from the parasession on natural phonology*, pp.346-374. Chicago Linguistic Society, University of Chicago.

WEIGL, E. and M. Bierwisch. 1970. "Neuropsychology and linguistics: topics of common research." *Foundations of Language* 6:1-18.

WHITAKER, H.A. 1971. *On the representation of language in the human brain.* Edmonton, Alberta: Linguistic Research Inc.

_______________. 1972. "Unsolicited nominalizations by aphasics; the plausibility of the lexicalist model." *Linguistics* 78:62-71.

— announcing a new series in anthropology —

OTHER REALITIES

In Other Realities, *descriptive, methodological, and theoretical texts will be devoted to the exploration of new frontiers of contemporary anthropological research. Each society creates* a *reality in which its members live, feel and think. For them it is* the *reality, firmly existing out there, and the same for everybody. For anthropologists, who usually experience more than one society, realities are many, varied, and in the mind.*

On Linguistic Anthropology: Essays in Honor of Harry Hoijer, 1979

- **J. Greenberg:** "Universals of Kinship Terminology: Their Names and the Problem of Their Explanation"
- **D. Hymes:** "Tonkawa Poetics: John Rush Buffalo's 'Coyote and Eagle's Daughter'"
- **P. W. Friedrich:** "Linguistic Relativity and the Order-to-Chaos Continuum"

In 1978, the Department of Anthropology, UCLA, established a series of lectures both to honor the memory of Professor Harry Hoijer (1904-1976) and to give recognition to the original contributions of eminent scholars in the field. As Professor Hoijer's particular expertise was in the interface of culture and language, these first essays are devoted to the field of linguistic anthropology. Additional volumes of the Harry Hoijer lectures will appear regularly within the series *Other Realities.*

In *Other Realities* descriptive, methodological, and theoretical texts will be devoted to the exploration of new frontiers of contemporary anthropological research. Jacques Maquet, the editor of this series, is a professor in and the chairman of the Department of Anthropology at the University of California, Los Angeles.

LC: 80-50214 ISBN: 0-89003-062-6 Malibu: Undena Publications, 1980
140 pp. $12.00/hard, $9.00/paper

ALSO AVAILABLE

Introduction to Aesthetic Anthropology

Jacques Maquet — *Other Realities*, Vol. 1

This book is an anthropologist's attempt at understanding the visual arts from the cross-cultural and contextual vantage point of his discipline.

LC Card Number: 79-67375 ISBN: 0-89003-041-3 Malibu: Undena Publications, 1980
108 pp. $8.30/paper (second edition, revised)

Prepaid orders from individuals. Please order from
UNDENA PUBLICATIONS, P. O. Box 97, Malibu, CA 90265, U.S.A.

ARTANES

Aids and Research Tools in Ancient Near Eastern Studies

Editor: Giorgio Buccellati

A collection of practical volumes to be used in teaching and research in Ancient Near Eastern Studies, with the flexibility needed to accommodate diverse formats. Manuals, workbooks, dictionaries, bibliographies, exercise books, chronological tables and the like are some of the categories suitable for the series.

ARTANES 1

***ENGLISH-EGYPTIAN INDEX OF FAULKNER'S* CONCISE DICTIONARY OF MIDDLE EGYPTIAN**

by David Shennum

1977, pp., vi-178, $6.00/paper

This index is intended as a useful tool for locating textual material for comparative research in Egyptian semantics, history, archaeology and religion. While it is restricted to a given linguistic period, ample space has been provided for the user to insert his own lexical material from other stages of the language or to add notes and comments or otherwise to flesh out its contents for his own purposes.

ISBN 0-89003-054-5

ARTANES 2

IIMAS FIELD ENCODING MANUAL (NON-DIGITAL)

by Giorgio Buccellati and Marilyn Kelly-Buccellati

1978, pp., 52, $3.00/paper

The present manual is directed toward the specific needs of an ongoing operation at Terqa, Syria, but is meant for a more general application. It is both a working operation guide and archetype for a field recording system. The forms and arrangement provide for a uniform organization of the data with the establishment of discrete categories, consistency for matching preassigned slots, and cross-referencing function with numerous indices. Instructions for the use of the manual are succinct and in outline form. They are meant as an aid for the archaeologist in the field.

The IIMAS (International Institute for Mesopotamian Area Studies) Field Encoding Manual details the system's configuration, and explains the principles and elements of the stratigraphic and typological record. A special feature of the publication is the inclusion of 29 field forms.

ISBN 0-8900-3-058-8

ARTANES 3

A WORKBOOK OF CUNEIFORM SIGNS

by Daniel C. Snell

1979, pp., 140, $9.50/paper

This cuneiform workbook gives a course of programmed instruction teaching the 110 most frequently used signs. It teaches the standard Neo-Assyrian sign forms and gives the student practice both in passive and active recognition of the signs. The signs are divided into eight sections, and each section ends with a quiz reviewing all signs presented; appendices provide an alphabetic list of values taught and a list of the signs. The *Workbook* is designed for home study by students in beginning Akkadian classes and provides a practical introduction to the cuneiform writing system. It may be used in conjunction with R. Labat's *Manuel d'Epigraphie akkadienne* as well as the readings planned by the instructor.

ISBN 0-89003-058-8